HISTORICAL

FOOTNOTES[1]

‖ of ‖

LEBANON,

OHIO[2]

Best Wishes.

[1] Written by John J. Zimku‹

[2] Illustrated by Charlie Zimkus

ACKNOWLEDGMENTS

Mary Payne, museum director, and Mary Klei, curator, of the Warren County Historical Society for their help and for the use of the resources of the society's library — especially its extensive accumulation of microfilmed editions of *The Western Star*

Tom Barr, editor of *The Western Star*, for his support and permission to reprint the articles and pictures that originally appeared in the newspaper in slightly different form

Fred Compton, for sharing his recollections of Ronald Reagan's visit to The Golden Lamb

Paul Resetar, managing partner of The Golden Lamb Inn, for imparting his role in inviting President George W. Bush to visit Lebanon

The Cincinnati Historical Society Library, for permission to print excerpts from Edwin Forrest's poem "The Stranger's Death"

Key Metts, a friend and colleague, for her skill in proofreading this manuscript

Second printing, 2006

ISBN 0-9726224-0-3

These stories, with the exception of President Bush's visit, previously have been published in *The Western Star* from December 2001 through December 2002.

This book was printed by Sheridan Books in Ann Arbor, Michigan.

*To my wife, Pat for her love, patience and support,
and for her understanding that "research is neat."*

*And to my son and collaborator, Charlie, whose
talent, wit and warm heart have been a tremendous
source of pride for his parents.*

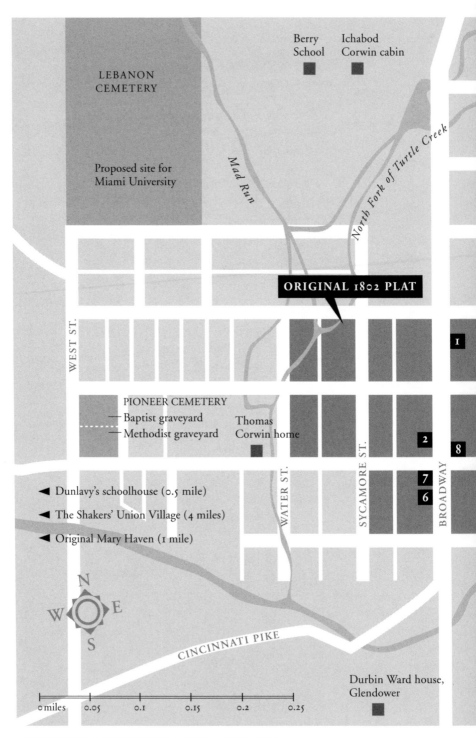

Berry School

Ichabod Corwin cabin

LEBANON CEMETERY

Proposed site for Miami University

Mad Run

North Fork of Turtle Creek

ORIGINAL 1802 PLAT

WEST ST.

1

PIONEER CEMETERY
— Baptist graveyard
---- Methodist graveyard

Thomas Corwin home

SYCAMORE ST.

2

8

◀ Dunlavy's schoolhouse (0.5 mile)

◀ The Shakers' Union Village (4 miles)

◀ Original Mary Haven (1 mile)

WATER ST.

BROADWAY

7
6

N
W E
S

CINCINNATI PIKE

Durbin Ward house, Glendower

0 miles   0.05   0.1   0.15   0.2   0.25

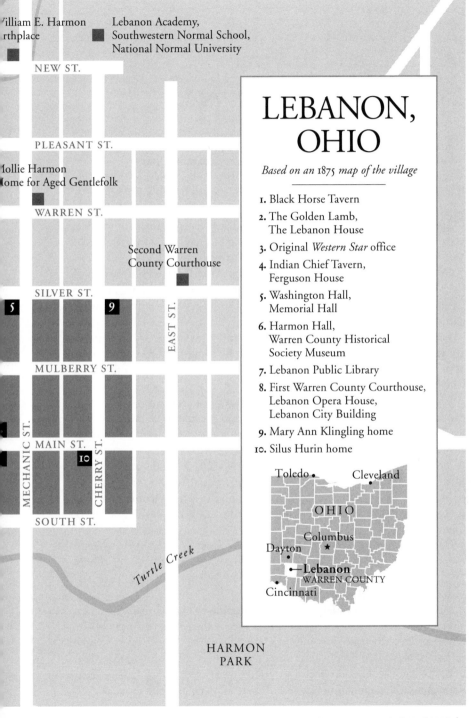

William E. Harmon
Birthplace

Lebanon Academy,
Southwestern Normal School,
National Normal University

NEW ST.

PLEASANT ST.

Hollie Harmon
Home for Aged Gentlefolk

WARREN ST.

Second Warren
County Courthouse

SILVER ST.

5   9

EAST ST.

MULBERRY ST.

MECHANIC ST.

MAIN ST.

CHERRY ST.

10

SOUTH ST.

Turtle Creek

HARMON
PARK

LEBANON, OHIO

Based on an 1875 map of the village

1. Black Horse Tavern
2. The Golden Lamb,
   The Lebanon House
3. Original *Western Star* office
4. Indian Chief Tavern,
   Ferguson House
5. Washington Hall,
   Memorial Hall
6. Harmon Hall,
   Warren County Historical
   Society Museum
7. Lebanon Public Library
8. First Warren County Courthouse,
   Lebanon Opera House,
   Lebanon City Building
9. Mary Ann Klingling home
10. Silus Hurin home

Toledo   Cleveland

OHIO

Columbus
Dayton   ★

Lebanon
WARREN COUNTY
Cincinnati

I Arrival and survival of Lebanon's first citizen

Ichabod Corwin is credited as being the first pioneer settler in the unyielding wilderness of what would someday become Lebanon, Ohio.

Soon after his birth in New Jersey in 1767, his family moved to Kentucky. It was there that he eventually met and married Sarah Griffin of Washington County, Pennsylvania.

After General "Mad" Anthony Wayne's victory over the Indians at the Battle of Fallen Timbers in 1794 and the signing of the Treaty of Greenville in August 1795, the Ohio country was opened to settlement.

Corwin left Bourbon County, Kentucky, in March 1796 with his wife and their three children and settled on the west side of the North Fork of Turtle Creek. He had purchased the half-section of land that is now the northwest part of Lebanon.

There Corwin built a cabin within the primitive forest and its thick undergrowth of spice brush. He cleared — as best he could — about 12 acres for corn, planting around the stumps and the "big buck" trees he could not fell with his ax.

Within a year of settling in the Turtle Creek Valley, on August 25, 1797, Sarah gave birth to Eliza, their fourth child and the first to be born north of the Ohio River. Eliza died in 1822, the only one of the Corwins' 13 children to precede them in death.

Indians stole Corwin's horses before he could fully work his corn. To feed his growing family, and with the horses gone, he carried flour for the baking of bread from Christian Waldschmidt's mill on the Little Miami River. The mill was about 20 miles to the south, not far from present-day Milford, Ohio.

Corwin eventually returned to Kentucky by foot and purchased a yoke of oxen. Unfamiliar with how to work the animals, he hired a "Yankee," a man from New England, "to drive them to the plow." Corwin is said to have harvested 100 bushels of corn to the acre.

Moses Beldso Corwin, Ichabod and Sarah's oldest son, eventually became a U.S. Congressman from Urbana, Ohio. He recalled that first year in the Ohio country when he was only six: "I have a perfect recollection of how things looked at that time, of our suffering with the cold in the woods ... and of the Indians stealing our horses soon after we arrived, and of father's starting on foot to Cincinnati to buy oxen. These were my happiest days."

Corwin would become one of the four founding fathers of Lebanon and one of the village's primary boosters and builders. A monument commemorating the site of his first cabin sits today in front of the Berry School on Broadway.

Ichabod Corwin died on October 26, 1834, at age 67. His death was the result of an injury sustained when a horse kicked him in the head. He was buried in the Baptist Graveyard, what is now the northern portion of the Pioneer Cemetery.

His tombstone reads, "The deceased was the first settler on the place where Lebanon now stands — March, 1796."

2 Master Dunlavy teaches school on Christmas Day

Francis Dunlavy was an extremely stubborn and highly educated pioneer of the Ohio frontier. He was not only the first teacher in Warren County, but he was also the first in the entire Miami Valley.

Dunlavy was born on December 31, 1761, near Winchester, Virginia. He was the oldest son of Anthony and Hannah Dunlavy's eight children. In 1772, the family moved west of the Allegheny Mountains to the settlement of Catfish in Washington County, Pennsylvania.

Frontier settlers at this time were often drafted into the militia to protect their frontier communities. Young Francis served no fewer than eight times before the age of 21. The first began on October 1, 1776, while he was still 14 years old. On a few occasions he served as a substitute for his father.

Despite these interruptions, Francis received a fine classical education, graduating in 1790 from Dickinson College in Carlisle, Pennsylvania. At first he planned to enter the Presbyterian ministry. Scriptural differences, however, caused him not only to change his vocation to education, but also to leave the church and become a Baptist, "to the mortification of his parents."

In 1792 he moved to Columbia at the mouth of the Little Miami River in the Northwest Territory and opened a school. That same year he married a young widow named Mary Craig Carpenter. Together they would have eight children. Dunlavy and his family moved upriver to the Turtle Creek Valley in 1797. The next spring he started a log cabin school in what is now Lebanon.

The school was located north of the creek on what is now West Main Street, where Lebanon's water department is today. He taught only boys. The subjects included Latin and the higher mathematics, as well as the "common branches."

Christmas was not observed at this time as it is today. Schools rarely closed for the day. But on December 25, 1798, the young men of Master Dunlavy's school decided to have a holiday and lock their teacher out.

To Dunlavy the idea of "treating" his students did not set well. He tried to enter the school through the window but the students fought him off with sticks. Finally Dunlavy climbed upon the roof and came down the clay chimney!

There was school that Christmas Day.

One week later, on New Year's Day, the students recruited some friends who didn't attend Dunlavy's school to come to the school to help them lock their teacher out. The fireplace was ablaze and the door was barricaded with firewood. When Dunlavy approached, a great roar of defiance came from the little cabin.

Dunlavy coolly surveyed the situation. Slowly he walked over to the woodpile and hoisted a large green log upon his shoulder. After stepping back several paces, he rammed the door with such force that it broke into several pieces.

There was school that New Year's Day.

Dunlavy left teaching at his old log cabin school in 1801 after he was elected to the Northwest Territorial Legislature. The new teacher was David Spinning, who, when locked out by his students, "treated" them to a gallon of stew.

3 Carved from the forest, a new town is born

Lebanon, Ohio, was laid out in September 1802. Ichabod Halsey was hired to survey the land by Ichabod Corwin, Ephraim Hathaway, Silus Hurin and Samuel Manning. One hundred lots were carved out of a virgin woods with a dense ground cover of spice brush.

These thickets were almost impenetrable. They had yellow flowers that appeared in early spring. By September small clusters of berries ripened to a deep red and were often used in place of allspice. Boiling the leaves made a stimulating drink that could fight fevers, giving the shrub the added name of "fever bush."

Among the many types of trees were white oak, black walnut, elm and sycamore.

The town, cradled between Turtle Creek and its North Fork, was to be 4½ blocks long and a mere 3 blocks wide, but was currently home to only two cabins.

Corwin built a two-story hewed log cabin in 1800 on what is now the east side of Broadway between Mulberry and Silver streets. It was the first building within the original borders of Lebanon. It was there that Corwin's daughter Lucinda was born on December 8, 1800. She eventually would marry Francis Dunlavy's son, Anthony Howard.

Just a few days earlier, on November 27, Catherine Hurin was born in a cabin erected by her father, Silus. Their home was on Cherry Street just south of Main. The girls were the first two children born in what became Lebanon.

Although there were several streets and alleys on the original map, only two were named: Broadway and Main. Broadway was always intended to be a "broad way." It was "6 poles wide," a pole being 5½ yards long. All the other streets were measured at 4 poles. It is believed Broadway was made this wide so that a stagecoach could make a U-turn on it without difficulty.

The boundaries of the first Lebanon were Silver Street to the north, South Street to the south, Water Street to the west, and the alley between Cherry and East streets to the east. The original plat excluded the southwest corner of its rectangle due to swampy land.

Three of the founders hoped to build the town a little farther north on higher ground. Samuel Manning, however, who owned this land, was reluctant to

offer it. He believed the town would not succeed, stating that "it would never be anything but a nest of thieves."

The four corners at the intersection of Broadway and Main were set aside as the town square. Corwin owned the land northwest of the square, Hathaway the land to the northeast and Hurin the south side of the crossroads. Manning's contribution, which was in the northeast section of the plat, was small in comparison.

Although the survey was made in September 1802, it was not filed until a year later on October 18, 1803. It was the seventh document received by the Warren County Recorder's office.

On January 9, 1810, the town of Lebanon was officially incorporated.

4 First things first: The Black Horse Tavern

At one time the Black Horse Tavern practically was Lebanon, Ohio.

Ichabod Corwin built the two-story hewed log cabin to be his family's new home in 1800. It was located on the east side of Broadway between Mulberry and Silver streets.

The Corwins lived there for only about two years. Corwin sold it and approximately 15 surrounding acres to Ephraim Hathaway. Corwin then moved back to his original cabin, where the Berry School is today.

Hathaway was from Redstone, Pennsylvania. When he and his brother first traveled to the Ohio country by flatboat down the Ohio River, they were ambushed by Indians. Hathaway's brother was killed and the attack left Ephraim with a crippled right arm and an undying hatred of Indians.

Hathaway took Corwin's cabin and opened a tavern under the sign of the Black Horse. After the town of Lebanon was laid out in September 1802, the historical significance of the Black Horse began to multiply rapidly.

Since there were only two cabins on the original 100 lots of Lebanon, and it was the first built, it was naturally the first cabin in Lebanon. It also was the first business. Since that business was a tavern, it was the first tavern.

When John Huston and his nephew, Isaiah Morris, came up from Columbia at the mouth of the Little Miami River in June 1803, he rented a room from Hathaway on the first floor. There he established the first store in Lebanon in the Black Horse. It didn't last long, however. Huston soon died leaving Morris in financial trouble.

On March 24, 1803, an act of the Ohio General Assembly established Warren County. The act took effect on May 1, the county's first day of operation. Nine days later, Lebanon, because of its central location, was selected as the temporary county seat.

The acting courthouse was to be "the house of Ephraim Hathaway on Turtle Creek," making the Black Horse the first courthouse in Warren County.

The first court session took place on the third Tuesday of August 1803 at the Black Horse. There were several indictments for assault and battery, and disturbing the peace, but none of the cases went to trial.

The first trials took place in the next session in December 1803. One civil case and one criminal case for assault and battery were heard. The first paneled jury included Ichabod Corwin and Samuel Manning. One case in 1805 concerned the theft of Hathaway's buckskin money pouch.

The accused pleaded guilty and was sentenced to "three lashes on his naked back."

Hathaway served as Warren County's second sheriff from 1806 to 1810. As for the Black Horse, it lasted until 1826 when Hathaway tore it down and replaced it with a brick building, upon which he put the iron letters "E H."

Hathaway died of cholera on July 30, 1833, and was buried in the Baptist Graveyard.

Today The Golden Lamb Inn in Lebanon has a bar called Black Horse Tavern where visitors can enjoy a drink and a meal. On its wall are the same iron initials "E H."

5 The teacher who helped topple a governor

By November 1802, General Arthur St. Clair had ruled the wilderness north of the Ohio River for 14 years as governor of the Northwest Territory. St. Clair, however, had little faith in the pioneering settlers who were pouring into the territory. He believed that order must come before freedom and that he was the one to provide the order.

St. Clair had fought against the formation of the territorial legislature and now he was against the constitutional convention that was meeting in Chillicothe, the territorial capital. The purpose of the convention was to write a constitution for the new state of Ohio.

One who politically opposed St. Clair was a former teacher from the Turtle Creek Valley, in what was then part of Hamilton County. In 1800 he was elected to the territorial legislature and in 1802 was the county's top vote-getter for a seat at the constitutional convention. He was Francis Dunlavy, and he would play a significant role in the removal of St. Clair as governor of the Northwest Territory.

During the last session of the legislature in Chillicothe, a mob had assembled to loudly protest the proposed boundaries of Ohio.

The next day, three of the representatives from Hamilton County — Edward Foster, future Ohio governor Jeremiah Morrow, and Francis Dunlavy — were meeting.

Suddenly St. Clair entered the room and very bluntly attributed the mob's actions to political disputes. He went on to enumerate the problems of America's democratic institutions, stating that they could not last. Finally he remarked that the country needed to turn to a stronger government like that of England, which was, in his opinion, a model to all.

After St. Clair left, Dunlavy and the others sat in stunned silence.

Dunlavy then took pen in hand and wrote down everything the governor had said as the others looked on. After the three men signed the document in front of a justice of the peace, Dunlavy had it sent to President Thomas Jefferson.

On November 22, 1802, during the Ohio Constitutional Convention, word came from Washington that Jefferson was immediately dismissing St. Clair as governor of the Northwest Territory and appointing Charles William Byrd of Hamilton acting governor.

None of the three men ever publicly talked about their role in the matter.

Only after the death of both Foster and Dunlavy, did Dunlavy's son, Anthony Howard, learn from Morrow of his father's involvement. The younger man recalled, "Then the last, Governor Morrow, communicated it to me, as no longer necessary to be kept unexplained."

Francis Dunlavy died on November 6, 1839.

Although he was the first teacher in the Miami Valley and for 14 years served as a president judge in southwestern Ohio, his marker in Lebanon's old Baptist Graveyard does not mention these accomplishments.

What it does say is, "He was among the first white men to enter the Territory now forming Ohio; was a member of the Territorial Legislature; and of the Convention which formed the Constitution of Ohio."

6 The birth of Ohio's oldest inn: The Golden Lamb

Approximately 1,000 spectators crowded about Broadway on Saturday, April 27, 1940, for the unveiling of a plaque declaring The Golden Lamb as the "oldest hotel in Ohio." The festive scene was in sharp contrast to the venerable inn's more humble beginnings.

On December 23, 1803, Jonas Seaman spent $4 at the Black Horse Tavern, the county's temporary courthouse, for a license "to keep a house of Public Entertainment." His two-story log cabin was on lot No. 58 in Lebanon. It was next to the town square on Broadway on land Seaman had bought from Ichabod Corwin.

Seaman was no stranger to innkeeping. His father, William, ran a tavern in Hopewell, New Jersey, about 12 miles north of Trenton. Seaman's family had been in the Ohio country since 1790 and had lived in the Turtle Creek Valley since 1798. Now Seaman had his tavern, with its chicken coop, pig pen, small garden and stable.

It was during this time period that Seaman named his tavern The Golden Lamb. Since many pioneer settlers could not read, it was common to have a colorful sign of a recognizable object to identify a business. It could be a sign of a green tree, a red lion, a black horse or even a golden lamb.

In the tavern's first years when Seaman's wife, Martha, rang the dinner bell, she would provide their customers with meals of deer, bear or wild turkey with cornbread on the side. The food would be served on wooden or pewter plates on long communal tables.

As Lebanon's pioneer ways quickly disappeared, so did the rustic feel of the tavern. The wild game was replaced by more domestic fare served on Queensware at six smaller tables.

As at most of the inns of the day, patrons did not receive a menu but rather whatever food Martha prepared. Twenty-five cents was a typical price for a meal. Keeping the traveler's "horse at hay" was about the same price. As for lodging, a cozy spot in a bed was about half that amount. If the guest was more particular and wanted a private room, the price would go up sharply.

Although business grew after the permanent courthouse was opened across Broadway in 1806, Seaman found himself in financial difficulty. Lawsuits that year were brought against a number of settlers, including Seaman, for payment still owed on their land. Seaman in turn sued many of those who were in debt to him. Despite all his efforts, Seaman was forced in 1809 to hold

a public sale to satisfy his creditors and he soon relinquished ownership of his tavern.

Although Jonas Seaman faded from Lebanon's recorded history after 1819, the legacy of what he began continued to grow.

Today the Lebanon Room in The Golden Lamb marks the spot where his log cabin tavern once stood.

As for The Golden Lamb itself, its charm and traditional American menu continue to attract thousands of travelers and townspeople alike as Ohio's oldest inn.

7 A visit from three mysterious strangers

On March 22, 1805, three men dressed in black and wearing broad-brimmed hats arrived at the home of Malcham Worley in the pioneer community of Turtle Creek, four miles west of Lebanon. Worley was an active member of the Turtle Creek Church, once the largest and most influential Presbyterian church in the Symmes Purchase. In June 1804, the church members, under the leadership of their dynamic minister, the Rev. Richard McNemar, broke away from the Presbyterians and affiliated with a group called the "New Lights." Now the congregation, influenced by the three mysterious strangers, would go in another direction. This time Worley would take the lead.

The three men were John Meacham, Benjamin S. Young and Issachar Bates. They were brethren of the United Society of Believers in Christ's Second Appearing, more commonly known as Shakers. They had heard of the Great Kentucky Revival of 1800-03, where preachers, including the Rev. McNemar, filled the open meadows of Kentucky with such a high pitch of "fire and brimstone" as to bring their listeners to physical convulsions. Curious about the similarities between their "shaking" and the "jerks" that overcame the revivalists, the Shakers walked from their home in Mt. Lebanon, New York, to Kentucky.

Finding little success, they headed north to Ohio. Bates later wrote, "At Turtle Creek we found the first rest for the souls [sic] of our feet, having traveled 1,233 miles in two months and 22 days." After talking for a long time to Worley and the Rev. McNemar, the three Shakers were invited to church services the next Sunday.

They told of the prediction their founder, Ann Lee, had made that "the next opening of the gospel will be in the Southwest …." They explained the Shaker beliefs of a dual God (male and female), of the separation of the sexes, Christian communism, confession of sins and the separation from the world. Finally, after three days, the congregation realized that "the strangers offered not only a new belief but a new life."

Malcham Worley, according to some Shaker historians, was "a deep thinker on great themes, intensely and actively interested in religious matters." A non-Shaker observer, however, had the opinion that Worley's "excitable temperament had led him into such wild exercises during the revival that many doubted his sanity."

On March 26, Worley summoned McNemar to his home for a conference

with the strangers. In front of his wife and nine children, Worley listened and watched through the night. Early the next morning, according to Shaker historians, Worley stood and said, "Brethren, are you there?" To which the Shakers replied, "We are." Then, grasping their hands, he stated, "All I have is yours!"

Thus on March 27, 1805, Malcolm Worley became the first Shaker convert in the West. Within days, most of the Turtle Creek Church congregation, including the Rev. McNemar, also joined.

Union Village, as Warren County's Shaker settlement would be called, would last for more than 100 years, grow to 4,005 acres and, with 600 members at its height, be the second largest Shaker community in the United States.

8 'The Western Star:' A lucky beginning on Friday the 13th

Twenty-one-year-old John McLean drove an ox cart to Cincinnati in July 1806, to pick up an old Ramage printing press that had been brought to the river town in 1793. The press had an oak frame and a bed of stone. McLean's ambition was to be a lawyer, but now he was going to explore another profession. He was going to be the editor and publisher of a new newspaper: *The Western Star.*

Born in Morris County, New Jersey, on March 11, 1785, McLean was four when his family moved west. After relocating several times, they settled in what is now the community of Ridgeville in north central Warren County in 1799.

The printing press was set on the second floor of a house east of Broadway on the south side of Main Street in Lebanon, a half block from the town square.

On Friday, February 13, 1807, the first issue of *The Western Star* was published. Three hundred copies were made of the four-page paper. A subscription cost $2 per year or $2.50 per year if only half was paid in advance.

The "news" wasn't very new. There were reports on what had happened in Congress in December and on what Napoleon was doing in Europe in October.

The local ads included George Miller's "notice" that he now "carries on the cabinet making business, on Main Street, near Mr. Seaman's tavern," The Golden Lamb.

Ichabod B. Halsey, the man who had first mapped out Lebanon in 1802, had an ad printed with the heading, "Five Dollars Reward—Stop the Villain!" It seems he had taken in and clothed a young man "out of humanity." In return he was going to be paid with the teenager's "labour [sic] ... but like a thief, left [his] house in the night."

The last page of the paper included a poem. It began:

"The Western Star *now ushers forth*
From Lebanon, the seat of worth —
The news of consequence to give,
When we intelligence receive.
The interest of Ohio's land,
Shall ever be the greatest end —
To watch her rights with jealous care,
Is the first object of the Star.*"

McLean was admitted to the bar in 1807, the same year he began *The Western Star*. By 1810 he had sold the paper to his brother Nathaniel and decided to try his hand at politics. His quest eventually led him to a seat on the U.S. Supreme Court and a run for the U.S. presidency.

The old Ramage press stayed in Lebanon for nearly 60 years, long after it stopped being used. In the mid-1860s it was sold and sent out West to once again be the source of information in a pioneer community.

Today, *The Western Star*, despite beginning on Friday the 13th, has had the good fortune of becoming the oldest weekly newspaper still publishing in Ohio.

9 Lebanon, Ohio: Home of Miami University?

The Ohio General Assembly, on February 17, 1809, passed a law stating that a university would be "established and instituted" in "that part of the country known by the name of John Cleves Symmes' Purchase." The legislature decreed that the school "shall be designated by the name and style of 'The Miami University.'"

By 1809, however, the land between the Little Miami and Great Miami rivers, which makes up the Symmes or Miami Purchase, was already settled or claimed. Finding a "college township" within the Purchase would not be easy.

Three commissioners were given the job of looking over southwestern Ohio for a site for the school. They were Alexander Campbell, the Rev. James Kilburn and the Rev. Robert G. Wilson. Several towns, including Cincinnati, Dayton, Hamilton and Yellow Springs, competed to be the location of this new seat of higher learning.

The commissioners were directed to meet in Lebanon on June 6, 1809. Wilson, however, became ill and could not come. The remaining two did, and fell in love with the growing frontier community. This was especially true after Ichabod Corwin, one of the town's founding fathers, offered to donate 41 acres to establish Miami University in Lebanon.

Corwin was going to give the high land behind his homestead north of town. Situated west of the small steam called Mad Run, it was what is now the majority of the Lebanon Cemetery.

One of the commissioners was so thrilled with Corwin's offer that he took out his hunting knife and carved "M.U.V." into a large white oak tree on the hill. The initials stood for "Miami Uni Versity." The old oak stood for many years near where Governor Thomas Corwin, Ichabod's nephew, is buried.

Wilson later visited Lebanon and, pleased with his fellow commissioners' choice, signed the recommendation. Representatives from the other sites, however, were not pleased, and loudly protested the selection.

The state legislature, to appease the complaining communities, did not follow the recommendation. Their official reason was that Wilson had not made the initial visit to Lebanon with the other two commissioners. Like a mother who tells her children that if they don't stop fighting over a toy no one will get to play with it, the Ohio General Assembly gave the university to none of the existing towns.

On February 10, 1810, the state legislature directed that a town be laid out in the roadless wilderness of northwestern Butler County. They declared that the town would be called Oxford and be the home of "The Miami University."

A history of Warren County written in 1882 states, "It has been the opinion of eminent lawyers that Miami University was legally located at Lebanon, and that the change of the site to a point outside the Miami Purchase was in violation of the intention and purpose of the original grant by Congress .... No attempt, however, has been made to remove the institution from Oxford."

10 The curious story of the Shaker curse

Almost from 1805, when they first came to Warren County, the Shakers of Union Village were viewed with suspicion. A lot of this distrust was fostered by *The Western Star* in Lebanon. The paper's attacks fueled violence and destruction directed toward the society. Many, however, believe the Shakers got their revenge by putting a curse on Lebanon.

The cause of the distrust of the Shakers was, to a great extent, brought on by one of their own basic beliefs: separation from "the world." People tend to fear what they do not know and the Shakers purposely avoided contact with the outside world. In addition, their practice of celibacy also seemed quite foreign to simple frontier farmers.

Neighboring settlers sold their land to the Shakers, not to help them, but to get away from them.

Several mobs marched on Union Village during its first 20 years. The largest one was on August 27, 1810. That June, *The Western Star* had printed an article stating that Shaker beliefs were opposed to the American way of life and that celibacy would depopulate the country. Among other claims were that the Shakers danced naked, whipped children and murdered when it served their cause.

Now, nearly 2,000 people, including several hundred mounted soldiers, made their way to the Shaker community. Only after a small committee from the mob searched Union Village and found no signs of injustice or cruelty, did they finally disperse.

It is under such circumstances that the "curse" on Lebanon took place.

When it actually happened is not clear. One source says 1817, while Hazel Spencer Phillips, the noted Warren County historian, wrote that it occurred "about 1820."

A Shaker brother had a heavenly vision commanding that a curse should be put on Lebanon for being the source of so much of the society's persecution. At the same time, a blessing should be placed on Dayton. A Shaker community was founded there in 1806, called Watervliet. The townsfolk of Dayton reportedly treated the Believers well.

Two Shakers, Francis Beedle and Richard McNemar, mounted horses and rode along Broadway in Lebanon waving their wide-brimmed hats calling out, "Woe on all prosecutors." Later that afternoon they reached Dayton and shouted, "Blessings on all kindly souls."

Shaker historian Edward Deming Andrews called it "a curious story" and said that "according to the tale the progress of Dayton dated from this event; convinced that a community blessed by 'holy men of God' would surely prosper, ... [people] moved into town."

It is a fact that in 1820 Lebanon and Dayton were about the same size, a little more than 1,000 inhabitants, with Lebanon slightly larger. But by 1840, Dayton had a population of 6,067 to Lebanon's 1,327, and by 1890, the difference was 61,220 to 3,174.

Some doubt it was because of the curse, while others question if there ever was a "curse." But all must agree it is "a curious story."

II The young actor and 'The Stranger's Death'

The Golden Lamb became the first theater in Lebanon when new proprietor Henry Share constructed a stage in the 1820s. He brought a variety of attractions to town in an attempt to increase business at the hotel. One performance, however, would be cut short due to the death of a total stranger.

The hotel featured everything from an Egyptian mummy to exotic birds. For two weeks in February 1824, a trained elephant performed. In May 1833, for two nights, conjoined brothers, born in Siam, could be seen. Named Chang and Eng, their fame was so great that people began to use the term "Siamese twins" to describe siblings in their condition.

A young actor named Edwin Forrest brought Lebanon its first theatrical troupe in August 1823. In 1826, at the age of 20, Forrest would debut in New York City as Othello and become an overnight sensation. With his dynamic voice and athletic approach to acting, he was the first true star of "the American theatre." Junius Brutus Booth, a friend and contemporary of Edwin Forrest, named one of his sons after the noted actor. Edwin Booth would eventually be considered the greatest American actor of the 19th century. A shadow, however, is cast over his place in history. It is that of his younger brother, and fellow thespian, the infamous John Wilkes Booth.

In 1823, Forrest was 17 and a virtual unknown. His traveling company was touring "the West." He was about to perform in Lebanon as Young Norval, the hero of John Home's "The Tragedy of Douglas; or The Noble Shepherd." The troupe was scheduled for several weekends. Patrons could take their seats at 5 p.m., with the play beginning an hour later. The price was 25 cents.

On the third Saturday, after notices had been posted, the performance was canceled. It was out of respect. A death had occurred in The Golden Lamb. *The Western Star* reported on August 16, 1823, that "Mr. James Armstrong, hatter, died after two weeks illness at Henry Share's Hotel. Dr. Ross attended him, an entire stranger, from Virginia."

Forrest spent his idle time that weekend in his room in The Golden Lamb. There he composed a poem titled "The Stranger's Death." It read in part:

"I saw the Stranger on his bed of death—
Sunk was his eyes, and hard he drew his breath,
His quivering lips paleness had overcast,
And in dread agony his teeth clench'd fast.

"Disease had now full skeleton'd his frame;
No soul did know him, or from whence he came:
A Stranger — friendless — in an unknown land,
His fer'rish limbs by stranger zephyrs fann'd. ...

"... Upon the coffin now the clay was thrown,
Sounding mortality with candid tone.
A shriek was heard, and turning quickly round,
I saw near to the grave extended on the ground,
A MANIAC howling requiem on the Stranger dead—
The only tear was that the Maniac shed."

12 And now a toast: 'Hail to the Indian Chief'

The Golden Lamb has had an impressive list of visitors throughout its long and illustrious existence. But the greatest collection of powerful and influential men Lebanon has ever seen once gathered at its competition: the Indian Chief Tavern.

On March 23, 1805, William Ferguson bought half a lot in the newly founded town of Lebanon from Ephraim Hathaway for $40.50.

The land was located on the north side of Main Street, half a block east of the town square. There he built a two-story frame house from which he operated the Indian Chief Tavern, or the Ferguson House as it was later known.

Ferguson became one of Lebanon's first merchants when he opened a store by the inn. At the same time, across an alley on the tavern's west side, the new Warren County Courthouse was being built. The courthouse faced Broadway and was located where Lebanon's city building is today.

Ferguson became Lebanon's first postmaster on April 1, 1805. Soon after, post-riders out of Cincinnati began to make their weekly stops at the inn. Their route took them as far north as Urbana then west to Piqua and finally south, passing through Dayton, Franklin and Hamilton before completing their circuit in Cincinnati.

A few years later the first stagecoach to go through the town, the Cincinnati-Sandusky line, pulled up in front of the Indian Chief.

In April 1814, Ferguson became a member of the board of directors of The Lebanon Miami Banking Company, the first bank in Warren County.

On Friday, July 22, 1825, the Ferguson House was the site of one of the greatest gatherings of political leaders Ohio had ever seen. The occasion was a dinner to celebrate the beginning of the Ohio and Miami Canal, which had been dedicated the day before in Middletown, 12 miles west of Lebanon.

Present at the dinner were DeWitt Clinton, "the Father of the Erie Canal" and governor of New York; Ethan Allen Brown, "the Father of the Ohio Canal" and former governor of Ohio; Jeremiah Morrow, the governor of Ohio; and William Henry Harrison, Ohio's U.S. senator and future president of the United States.

Also there, by the pure coincidence of misfortune, was Henry Clay, the U.S. secretary of state. He was en route with his family to Washington, D.C.,

when Eliza, his 12-year-old daughter, took ill. They were staying at the Ferguson House while she recovered.

Toasts were made at the dinner to the president and vice president, "the memory of Washington," the U.S. government, "the County of Warren and its worthy citizens," and the Ohio and Miami Canal. Each of the major figures present was also, individually, so honored. In all, some 20 toasts were offered.

William Ferguson died in Lebanon in 1831 at the age of 61. The Ferguson House, under different names and owners, continued to operate as an inn for many years.

On September 1, 1874, it was destroyed in a massive fire that also took its neighbor, the old courthouse.

¹³ Eliza Clay: 'Cut down in the bloom of a promising youth'

In February 1825, Henry Clay accepted President John Quincy Adams' offer to be his secretary of state. Clay believed the appointment would bring him one step closer to his dream of becoming president. Clay was wrong, and the year would turn out to be one of the most tragic in his life.

Clay's youngest daughter, Eliza, celebrated her twelfth birthday on July 5, at Ashland, their home in Lexington, Kentucky. Shortly thereafter, she and several members of her family left for Washington, D.C. Eliza and her parents traveled by private coach with her older sister, Anne; Anne's husband, James Erwin; and her younger brothers, James, 6, and John, 4.

The Clay family arrived at the Ferguson House on Main Street, on July 15. By this time, however, Eliza was quite ill with typhoid fever. Caused by poor sanitary conditions, typhoid fever was a fairly common ailment at the time.

A Lebanon doctor advised the Clays to stay in town until Eliza was better, which he assured them would be in a few days. Weeks passed, however, and Eliza's condition showed little improvement.

Finally, on Sunday, August 7, after receiving assurances from the doctor that Eliza would recover but still needed rest, Clay left for Washington alone. Clay arrived two weeks later on Sunday, August 21. That morning at breakfast, he read in a Washington newspaper that Eliza was dead. She had died on Thursday, August 11, four days after he had left her.

Back in Lebanon, Eliza Clay's body had been placed in a narrow, black walnut coffin. She was buried in the Baptist Graveyard.

Clay had a limestone sarcophagus built. It was approximately 3 feet tall and 6 feet long. The inscription on the upper tablet read "Eliza H. Clay, daughter of Henry and Lucretia Clay who died on the 11th day of August 1825. Cut down in the bloom of a promising youth, while traveling through Ohio, hence from Lexington, Kentucky to Washington City. Her parents, who have erected this monument to her memory, console themselves with the hope that she now abides in heaven."

By the 1880s, the old Baptist Graveyard had become neglected. Rubbish had rapidly accumulated and a thick underbrush was allowed to clamber over the cemetery without hindrance. Students from the National Normal University in Lebanon were vandalizing Eliza's tombstone in search of limestone samples for class.

On July 26, 1894, Eliza Clay's body was exhumed at the request of Mrs. John M. Clay, her youngest brother's widow. It was brought to the Lexington Cemetery just more than two miles west from Eliza's home, Ashland.

Across the narrow cemetery road from where she is buried, and within a handsome marble tomb, are the remains of her parents. Above their monument is a towering column topped by a 12½-foot statue of Henry Clay facing her grave. It gives the impression that Eliza's father is now watching over her.

14 No brandy or parade for Charles Dickens

Of all the distinguished guests to stay at The Golden Lamb, only one, Charles Dickens, has the honor of having his name on two rooms, a guest room and a dining room. Quite a feat, considering there was no love lost between the acclaimed English novelist and Lebanon when he visited in 1842.

The Charles Dickens of 1842 was not the balding, mature gentleman with the Vandyke beard who most picture. This Dickens was just shy of 30, slender and clean-shaven, with long, dark brown hair that covered his ears in ringlets. Although some of his greatest works were yet to come, Dickens was famous in America. *Pickwick Papers, Oliver Twist* and *Nicholas Nickleby* had all been published before the end of 1839.

He arrived in Boston on January 22, 1842 with his wife, Catherine, and her maid. Together with a traveling secretary, they toured the country for five months. Dickens kept a journal of his trip, which became the basis of his book *American Notes*, published that October.

After touring as far west as St. Louis, they headed back east. At 8 a.m. on April 20, they boarded a mail coach in Cincinnati for Columbus. Dickens liked the Ohio landscape, calling it "a beautiful country." His opinion of coach drivers, however, was considerably lower.

"He is always dirty, sullen, and taciturn," Dickens wrote. "He always chews and always spits, and never encumbers himself with a pocket-handkerchief. The consequence to the box passenger, especially when the wind blows toward him, are not agreeable."

Dickens' coach arrived at 1 p.m. at The Bradley House, as The Golden Lamb was then known. Dickens wrote: "We dine soon afterwards with the boarders in the house, and have nothing to drink but tea and coffee. As they are both very bad and the water is worse, I ask for brandy; but it is a Temperance Hotel, and spirits are not to be had for love or money. This preposterous forcing of unpleasant drinks down the reluctant throats of travelers is not at all uncommon in America."

After the meal there was a change of coaches. Dickens' party continued its journey all night, arriving in Columbus just before 7 a.m.

Lebanon's feelings toward Dickens were likewise less than cordial. As *The Western Star* reported on April 22, "Mr. Dickens and lady passed through this place on Wednesday, ... and we have been gratified to observe the total

absence of all that parade and sycophancy which characterized his reception in the Eastern cities. It will give us a better opinion of ourselves, if even Mr. Dickens should not think the better of us for it."

Dickens solidified his position as the most popular writer of his time when he published *A Christmas Carol* in December 1843. In it he described Scrooge as "hard and sharp as flint, from which no steel had ever struck out generous fire," characteristics perhaps inspired by his treatment in a stage-stop town amidst the "beautiful country" of Ohio.

15 A stop on the Underground Railroad

The Underground Railroad was a loose network of free blacks, abolitionists, Quakers and other groups who assisted slaves in escaping to the North. Wilbur H. Siebert is recognized as its greatest authority. His 1898 book, *The Underground Railroad: From Slavery to Freedom*, includes a map showing a route of the Underground Railroad splintering into three directions after leading to Lebanon.

The term "Underground Railroad" was coined when a slave, Tice Davids, escaped across the Ohio River in 1831. His frustrated master said Davids "must have gone off on an underground road." As the story was repeated, the word "road" was replaced by a new means of transportation: the railroad.

Hundreds of escaped slaves passed through Warren County but their exact number, the locations of all the "stations" and the names of many "station masters" will never be known. Sometimes circumstantial evidence provides the only clues.

In 1941 Jesse Wilson, an elderly black man, informed the newly formed Warren County Historical Society that Governor Thomas Corwin's home on Main Street had been a "station." Wilson's parents worked for the Corwins, and he recalled being told that runaways hid in the attic of the 1818 house.

Some believe Francis Dunlavy's home on East Main Street also was a "station." Dunlavy was a lifelong abolitionist. While helping to write the Ohio Constitution in 1802, he voted to strike out the word "white," giving the right to vote to all free men. He was unsuccessful.

R. G. Corwin, son of Lebanon founder Ichabod Corwin and a cousin to Thomas, wrote to Siebert in 1895 about how his old home, located on the present-day site of the Berry School, was used to hide slaves. "My first recollection of the business dates back to about 1820, when I remember seeing fugitives at my father's house," he wrote, "though I dare say it had been going on long before that time."

"Conductor" John Van Sandt often drove runaways to Lebanon. On April 23, 1842, slave catchers stopped him north of Cincinnati and caught seven slaves. An eighth escaped. Van Sandt was arrested and fined $1,200. He was the inspiration for the character "John Van Thrompe" in Harriet Beecher Stowe's *Uncle Tom's Cabin*, published in 1851.

Aiding runaways was costly for Van Sandt, but it was especially dangerous for free blacks — it could cost them their freedom. Unfortunately, the

accounts of black "station masters" are sorely lacking and often overlooked. A house on New Street, owned by free blacks, reportedly had a hidden tunnel to hide slaves.

Much of what is known about the Underground Railroad is clouded by myth and mystery. Secrecy was vital to its success and knowing too much could put the whole network in jeopardy. "Station masters" often only knew the next stop north on the route.

Many former slaves in Canada refused to reveal the names of those who aided them in their flight to freedom. They had promised that they never would. And they never did.

16 Senator Thomas Corwin's courageous speech

On Sunday, May 9, 1965, an episode of the NBC anthology television series *Profiles in Courage* aired. Based on President John F. Kennedy's 1957 Pulitzer Prize-winning book, the series had been planned before the president's death. It was his idea to expand the program beyond his book, and tell the stories of "other Americans who displayed extraordinary personal courage." This particular episode was about Senator Thomas Corwin from Lebanon, Ohio.

Corwin was born in Bourbon County, Kentucky, on July 29, 1794. In 1798 his father, Matthias, brought his family north into the Ohio Territory. They followed Matthias' brother, Ichabod, to the future site of Lebanon. Young Tom studied law in the office of Joshua Collett, Lebanon's first lawyer. By 1817 he was admitted to the bar and quickly entered politics. Over the next 25 years he served as prosecuting attorney for Warren County, a member of the Ohio General Assembly, a U.S. congressman and governor of Ohio. In the fall of 1844, he was elected to the U.S. Senate.

In March 1845, Congress passed the Texas annexation resolution, which drew the new state's border with Mexico at the Rio Grande. Mexico disagreed, claiming that the boundary was 150 miles farther north at the Nueces River. On April 25, 1846, fighting broke out between the neighboring countries.

On February 11, 1847, Corwin put his political career on the line and rose in the Senate to speak against an appropriations bill to supply American soldiers in the field. Corwin questioned whether the fighting was actually over U.S. soil. He read a portion of a letter from an officer in the disputed territory. The soldier wrote that he was "right in the enemy's country" where the people were "leaving their homes" as the American troops approached.

Corwin asked, "What is the territory, [President Polk], which you propose to wrest from Mexico? ... His Bunker Hills, and Saratogas, and Yorktowns are there!" Corwin predicted a war over slavery, stating that if "a single acre of Mexican land" is taken, "the North and South are brought into collision on a point where neither will yield."

"The Senator from Michigan says ... we want room," Corwin said. "If I were a Mexican I would tell you, 'Have you not room in your own country to bury your dead men? If you come to mine, we will greet you with bloody hands, and welcome you to hospitable graves.'"

Corwin closed his 2½-hour speech by pleading, "Show Mexico that you are sincere when you say that you desire nothing by conquest." Afterwards Corwin was labeled a traitor by some newspapers and burned in effigy across the country.

The United States won the Mexican War, gaining one-third of Mexico's land, including what is now California and all or part of six other states.

The *Ohio State Journal* fairly observed on May 27, 1847, that Corwin was expressing "an earnest and impassioned advocacy of what he believed to be right against all odds and in face of all opposition."

¹⁷ Alfred Holbrook: 'Teacher of teachers'

A convention was held in 1855 at Miami University in Oxford, Ohio, to find a location for a normal school, or teacher's college, in southwestern Ohio. The site selected was Lebanon. The man chosen to head the school was an educational innovator: Alfred Holbrook.

The Southwestern Normal School, as it was first called, began on November 24, 1855, in the Lebanon Academy building on New Street.

Normal schools originated in Europe. The first American one was established in Massachusetts in 1839. The word "normal" refers to the "model or pattern" behaviors and skills a teacher will need to be effective.

Almost from the start, Holbrook and his school were controversial. The school was coeducational and women had the same freedom from supervision as men. There were no final exams and the lecture system of teaching was abandoned. Long days were filled with written assignments and numerous recitations by the students. There was no time for collegiate athletics. Summer vacations didn't exist.

An average four-year college program was arranged in two 50-week years. Classes were from Tuesday to Saturday. This allowed Sunday to be used for study and gave "the ladies a better opportunity for individual laundry work" on Monday, the traditional "wash day."

The university's academic reputation was so strong that graduates of Holbrook's Classic Course program could enter Yale University for their senior year without taking an entrance examination.

The school's name was changed in 1870 to the National Normal School. Eleven years later it adopted the name by which it was best known, the National Normal University. By this time, it was the largest normal school in Ohio, attracting nearly 4,000 students per year and occupying approximately a dozen buildings in Lebanon.

In 1886 Holbrook adopted the title of President of the University. When its designation as a "normal school" was dropped in 1907, it became Lebanon University.

The school attracted the kind of students who would strive to make a difference. They included Cordell Hull from Tennessee, Franklin D. Roosevelt's secretary of state and the "father of the United Nations;" Albert B. Graham, founder of the 4-H Club; Myers Y. Cooper, governor of Ohio from 1929 to 1931; Louisa Jurey Wright, Lebanon Public School's first and only female

superintendent, who served from 1867 to 1868; Henry S. Lehr, president and founder of Ohio Northern University; and beloved Lebanon teacher, Lucile Blackburn Berry.

Despite the school's academic success, it suffered financially. Holbrook is said to have "naive management practices," and he eventually was removed as its president. The university finally closed in 1917 when its records were turned over to Wilmington College in a "merger." By then, some 80,000 graduates had passed through Holbrook's college.

Holbrook died in 1909. He is buried in the Lebanon Cemetery. Behind a large family marker is a smaller stone with the words "President Alfred Holbrook."

A history of the National Normal University, written in 1928, rightfully referred to him as "the father of normalism in the middle west, ... Alfred Holbrook, teacher of teachers."

18 Washington Hall:
A building of all trades

If a building could receive therapy for having an identity crisis, Lebanon's Washington Hall would be a prime candidate. It served as everything from a school chapel to a veteran's hall, and from a fire department to a market house. To add to its confusion, it was created illegally.

It all began in 1855, when the village council decided to build a new market house. The old one had stood in the middle of Silver Street where it intersects with Mechanic. The new site was to be at the southwest corner of the same intersection, but a public vote on September 8 went against it. Proponents of the new hall then formed a joint-stock company to raise the money privately. The village became a stockholder, an illegal act. No court action, however, was taken against this marriage of private and public funds.

On December 24, 1856, the new hall was dedicated with a festival sponsored by the fire company. The stockholders christened the building Washington Hall on January 10.

The south side of the first floor was for the fire department, while the market hall occupied the north. Upstairs was an auditorium that could seat 500 people.

The first lecture at Washington Hall was by the Rev. C.C. Giles on January 23, 1857. The topic was "Humanity in the Nineteenth Century." Over the next 20 years, prominent dignitaries such as Horace Mann, Congressman Rutherford B. Hayes, James A. Garfield and Lebanon's own Thomas Corwin would speak there.

During Christmas of 1859, the ladies of the Methodist Protestant Church used the hall for a "festival." Evergreens and artificial flowers decorated Washington Hall as did well-placed cages of "Canary birds." It was reported that "the little fellows ... added to the mirth and glee."

The following year, the "Festival of Firemen" took place on December 22. Christmas could be a very rowdy time, so it was promised in *The Western Star* that "nothing will be permitted to enter the program which will offend the most fastidious ear or eye."

The upper floor was leased to the National Normal University in 1859, to be used as a chapel. In 1874, the village voted to repair the hall but the decision was overturned in court. It decreed that the improvements would actually aid the school, a private entity, so public money could not be used.

After the Civil War, the market hall closed and the fire department took

over the entire lower level. A veterans post, organized in 1882, began to meet upstairs.

When the Opera House was built in 1878, Washington Hall's glory days were over. This new town hall had an auditorium nearly 2½ times larger. In the early 1900s, Washington Hall was renamed Memorial Hall because of its long association with veterans groups. However, by the 1950s, even the American Legion and the Veterans of Foreign Wars left for newer quarters.

The county, its owners by this time, had the very confused Washington Hall torn down in 1963.

¹⁹ Durbin Ward: Lawyer, soldier, man of principle

Durbin Ward always did what he believed was right rather than what was popular, despite the political consequences. It was said that "his firm adherence to principle ... often led to his defeat by less able men." This "adherence" also led him to support a president he had campaigned against, and become the first in Warren County to volunteer to fight in the Civil War in defense of the Union.

Ward was born in Augusta, Kentucky, in 1819. After attending Miami University for two years, he came to Lebanon and studied law under Thomas Corwin. In 1842 Ward became Corwin's law partner. He was elected prosecuting attorney in 1845 and won election as a Democrat to the Ohio legislature in 1851. He campaigned unsuccessfully for the U.S. Congress and the Ohio attorney general's office in the late 1850s. In 1860 Ward attended the Democratic Convention and actively supported Stephen A. Douglas for president over Abraham Lincoln.

On April 15, 1861, Ward was involved in a trial at the Warren County Courthouse when word came that President Lincoln was asking for 75,000 volunteers. Fort Sumter had been attacked three days earlier, igniting the Civil War.

Ward is said to have taken out a piece of paper and written, "We, the undersigned, hereby tender our services to the President of the United States to protect our national flag." He then signed it and continued with the trial.

The next night there was a war meeting at Washington Hall. "I shall never forget that meeting," a participant recalled. "Durbin Ward made a brief terse speech, eloquent for its simplicity .... A paper which he had drawn up, ... was passed from hand to hand and many names were written upon it. ... The meeting was solemn throughout, and ... the audience dispersed as quietly as a congregation leaving a church after listening to an impressive sermon."

Ward enlisted as a private, but, by August 17, was serving as a major in the 17th Ohio Volunteer Infantry. By September 1863, he was a lieutenant colonel and involved in the fighting at Chickamauga, Georgia. There he was severely wounded, forever losing the use of his left arm.

He was mustered out of the army but fought to have the order recalled. He succeeded and remained in the military until October 1865, when he was discharged with the honorary commission of brigadier general. Ward

continued to be politically active. He served as U.S. district attorney for southern Ohio and in the Ohio Senate, but lost his second try at Congress.

Durbin Ward died on May 22, 1886. Among the scores of monuments at the Chickamauga and Chattanooga National Military Park in Georgia is one for him.

His tombstone in the Lebanon Cemetery is not easy to find. It is a small, simple military marker like the thousands found at Arlington or Gettysburg. It may not have been the popular choice in which to honor him, but for Durbin Ward, principle was more important than popularity.

20 'There is but one Corwin!'

Accounts of Thomas Corwin's political career always refer to his eloquence as a public speaker. His skill during political campaigns — due in no small measure to his indomitable wit — singled him out as the unofficial "king of the stump."

In 1821, Corwin was serving in the Ohio legislature and supported a bill that would outlaw public whippings in Ohio. Another member of the Ohio General Assembly, who was originally from Connecticut, opposed the bill. This gentleman said that after a man was whipped in his old state he would immediately leave it. Whereupon Corwin rose and said, "I know a great many people have come to Ohio from Connecticut, but I have never before known the reason for their coming."

While serving in the U.S. Senate in the mid-1840s, Corwin was cornered in the halls of the Capitol by a rather pompous senator who reveled in quoting long passages of his own speeches. After finishing a particularly long excerpt from one of his orations, the senator said, "Why if I didn't have so many irons in the fire, I'd publish every one of my speeches for posterity."

"Take my advice, Senator," Corwin said, as he escaped from his colleague, "and put your speeches where your irons are!"

Another story of Corwin's famed wit may be more fable than fact but was still told quite often in the halls of Congress. It concerns the powerful John C. Calhoun of South Carolina and Congressman Corwin. The two were observing a drove of Ohio mules moving through Washington.

Calhoun remarked, "There go some of your constituents."

To which Corwin reportedly replied, "Yes, they are going down South to teach school."

Corwin's humor often focused on his family. In the late 1840s his only son, William Henry, was attending what is now Dennison University in Granville, Ohio. In a letter to him, Corwin wrote, "I am informed that you are seriously injuring your health by studying. Very few men nowadays are likely to be injured in this way but if you should kill yourself by overstudying, it will give me great pleasure to attend your funeral."

Despite his long and varied career, Corwin was convinced in his older years that his life was a failure. He attributed this failure to his love of humor.

After observing a young speaker joking with his audience, he said, "Don't do it, my boy. You should remember the crowd always looks up to the ring-

master and down on the clown. ... If you would succeed in life you must be solemn, solemn as an ass. All the great monuments of earth have been built over solemn asses."

Even on December 18, 1865, the night he died of a stroke, Corwin and his wit were once again the center of attention. Corwin was at a social gathering of governmental and military dignitaries in Washington. An eyewitness described those last, fleeting, jovial moments:

"Some sat, some stood, some kneeled, and all leaned forward to listen. ... His youth, with its inimitable charms and graces, seemed for a moment to have come to him again. There were once more the flow of humor, the sparkle of merriment, the glow of enthusiasm, the flash of wit, and the charms of anecdote and illustration; and there the wondrous play of features which made him Corwin. Men came repeatedly out from his presence at that seat, that night, exclaiming, 'There is but one Corwin!'"

21 The mystery of Mary Ann Klingling

Today, few can identify the "Mary" of the Mary Haven Youth Center on Justice Drive. Some may have heard the name, but to most, even in her day, Mary Ann Klingling was a mystery.

She was born Marie Anna Klingling in Frankfort on the Main, Germany, in 1798. She came to America with her brothers. Her brother John Richard opened a drug store in 1837 on Lebanon's Broadway. After his death four years later, Mary inherited much of his estate and bought the house at 203 E. Silver Street.

Mary seemed eccentric to many folks. She was foreign-born and kept to herself, making the gossip about her even more tantalizing. They whispered about her supposed wealth and told stories of a failed romance back in Germany that resulted in her vow to never marry. They laughed at her clothes.

"Her peculiar dress, which may have been in vogue in Germany in a past generation, attracted to her considerable attention," reported *The Western Star*.

Judge William S. Mickle was one of the few people with whom she associated. The equally eccentric Mickle was a neighbor who lived alone with his parrot. One August day in 1867, they went on a buggy ride. The horse was spooked and the carriage overturned, resulting in her death on August 16.

A week later her will was made public. The vast majority of her estate was pledged to build an "Orphan Asylum" for "poor white children." She wanted it to "be in or near Lebanon," not be "controlled by any particular sect of Christians" and have a "like sum for the benefit of the institution" donated. She also requested that "children of German parentage" be treated fairly. If neither Lebanon nor Warren County had acted upon her request after six years, the estate would go to a German orphanage in Cincinnati.

The estate turned out to be worth $40,000, the equivalent of nearly $500,000 today.

The county commissioners accepted the bequest but felt it "advisable to make provisions for ... [all] indigent children," regardless of race.

On February 11, 1869, the Ohio legislature authorized the commissioners to build one structure to house two institutions. They required that "two sets of books" be kept, one for Mary's children's home and the other for an orphanage.

Thus, in 1874, the three-story Orphans' Asylum and Children's Home

was built. It was situated on 53 acres one mile west of Lebanon on what is now St. Rt. 63. For a century it was a safe "haven" for orphans, and was eventually called Mary Haven. By the mid-1970s, however, it became a home for delinquent children. In 1996 the name Mary Haven left the old home and was placed on the new facility on Justice Drive.

One mystery about Mary remains. She was buried in the old Methodist Graveyard in what is now part of the Pioneer Cemetery. At her request, there was no marker. In death, as in life, Mary Ann Klingling has kept to herself.

22 The dramatic death of Clement Vallandigham

Clement Vallandigham's life could provide the plots for a dozen novels. He was a journalist, a lawyer and a congressman. A leader among the "Copperheads" in opposition to the Civil War, he was convicted of treason and banished to the South. Vallandigham's death in Lebanon was no less dramatic.

An incident occurred on Christmas Eve of 1870, in an upstairs gaming room in Hamilton, Ohio. The antagonists "were both notorious thugs," but now one was dead and the other was charged with his murder. Thomas McGehan, the accused, claimed that Thomas Meyers, the victim, accidentally shot himself. Hatred for McGehan forced the trial to be moved to Lebanon. It began on June 6, 1871, with a dozen or more prominent lawyers involved with the case. Vallandigham was for the defense. He stayed at The Golden Lamb, or The Lebanon House as it was then called, in a room on the second floor overlooking Broadway.

On the evening of June 16, Vallandigham and two of his co-counsels, A. G. McBurney and Thomas Millikin, had just returned from nearby Turtle Creek. There they had fired a Smith & Wesson revolver to discover the proximity needed to produce powder burns on cloth. Millikin reminded Vallandigham that there were still three rounds in the revolver, but Vallandigham seemed unconcerned.

A package containing a new pistol was handed to Vallandigham to be used in his courtroom demonstration the following Monday. As he and McBurney entered his hotel room, he unwrapped it and put both guns on the bureau. It was approximately 9 p.m.

Vallandigham said, "I will show you how Myers handled his pistol and shot himself." He then picked up the wrong revolver. McBurney recalled that he "put it into the right-hand pocket of this pantaloons; then drew it out and when the muzzle was almost out of his pocket, the pistol discharged." McBurney remembered Vallandigham yelling something like, "Oh murder!"

McBurney ran for help. Several jurors, who were staying at the hotel, rushed in to find Vallandigham walking about the room tearing open his clothing.

"What a foolish thing to do," he said. Within minutes Drs. Scoville and Drake were at the scene. The startling news quickly spread through Lebanon.

Vallandigham had a telegram sent to his personal physician, Dr. J. C. Reeve. "I shot myself by accident with a pistol in the bowels. I fear I am fatally injured. Come at once." Dr. Reeve and Vallandigham's 16-year-old son, Charlie, arrived

from Dayton at about 1 a.m. Charlie sat at his father's bedside. Vallandigham stroked his son's hair affectionately, telling him, "Be a good boy, Charlie."

The defendant, McGehan, was brought into the room under guard at about 7 a.m. *The Western Star* reported that he had "always been represented as being cold and remorseless ... [but now he] could not repress his tears. They fell thick and fast."

By 9:45 a.m. Vallandigham's pulse was indiscernible. He labored for breath as he asked for ice and "more opiates" for the pain.

Vallandigham then died, completing his dramatic demonstration.

²³ Celebrating the 100th birthday of 'dear old Lebanon'

For three days in late September 1902, the people of Lebanon celebrated their town's 100th birthday. Through concerts, speeches, parades and fireworks they commemorated their village's illustrious past and the scene of its "struggles, triumphs [and] defeats."

The festivities began at 10 a.m. on Thursday, September 25, at the Opera House. Several dignitaries spoke that morning, including Senator Mark Hanna, Ohio Governor George K. Nash and Ohio Secretary of State Lewis C. Laylin.

The honor of giving the centennial oration went to professor William Henry Venable. Born in Warren County in 1836, he was educated at Lebanon's National Normal University. At the time, Venable ranked "among the first of Ohio's most honored educators and authors." He began his highly regarded speech by stating, "Lebanon! How pleasantly upon the ear falls the sound of the melodious, oriental word. There must have been a poetical strain in the sober-minded backwoodsmen who christened the town."

That night at the Opera House there was a "Centennial Musicale," featuring Lebanon-native and internationally renowned opera singer Laura Bellini.

Friday's celebration included an industry and flower parade. "Flowers by the thousands and miles of bunting were used," reported *The Western Star*. It probably wasn't an exaggeration because the parade included 85 floats and lasted nearly three hours.

The Kings Mills Band — "perhaps, the most famous band in Southern Ohio" — preceded the first float, sponsored by *The Western Star*. It had a gigantic star encircled by potted plants. "At the four corners and mounted on the star were five young ladies."

The Lebanon Patriot newspaper was represented by its editor and owner, Mrs. Mary V. Proctor Wilson. She drove a small carriage covered with pink roses, perhaps in preparation for Saturday's "exhibition of ladies driving on Broadway."

The Lebanon Farmers' Club had 30 of its members riding on a float seated at a banquet table surrounded by farm products. Their banner read, "We eat the best, and feed the rest."

Saturday's parade was smaller in comparison. It was for schools and fraternal organizations. Nearly 100 Civil War veterans either walked or rode wagons. Then came the Independent Order of Odd Fellows, or the I.O.O.F., followed by what was referred to as the "colored Odd Fellows."

"One of the very best features of the day" was the procession of members of Lebanon's Improved Order of Red Men lodge. In Indian costumes and with their faces "besmeared with war paint," they rode horses bareback.

Lebanon High School, which in those days was on Pleasant Street, had four floats. One was of a large floral bell. Students Frank O'Neall and Mary Dilatush were dressed as George and Martha Washington.

That night fireworks closed the Lebanon Centennial Celebration.

William Venable conveyed the mood of those three days in 1902 quite eloquently. "We have come together to talk over the by-gone, to recount the annals of the village — scene of our struggles, triumphs, defeats — theatre of our loves and our sorrows — your town, my town, dear old Lebanon."

²⁴ William Elmer Harmon: 'Serving one's own people'

By age 38, William Elmer Harmon had founded a real-estate firm that was considered the largest in the world. While Harmon spent the first half of his life amassing a great fortune, he devoted the second half to giving it away, starting with his hometown of Lebanon.

Harmon was born on March 26, 1862, on North Mechanic Street. After graduating in 1881 from Lebanon High School, he briefly attended the National Normal University. Harmon then enrolled at a medical school in Kentucky, where, in 1883, he married.

Harmon's life then tragically turned upside down. Within two years his father, mother and wife died and he was left in financial straits. Determined to recover, Harmon's plan for success was to "hit upon something that everybody wanted, make it possible for everybody to buy it, and then let everybody know I have it for sale. ... Then the inspiration came, ... land, that's what everyone would like to own."

Harmon went to Cincinnati and shared his plan with his brother, Clifford, and his uncle, Charles Wood. On December 14, 1887, they developed the Branch Hill subdivision south of Loveland, Ohio. Harmon was innovative. By applying the installment plan to real estate, more people could afford to buy land. Branch Hill soon sold out and the firm of Wood, Harmon & Co. expanded rapidly. Over time offices opened in Pittsburgh, Boston, New York and 33 other cities.

Harmon married again in Boston and eventually moved his young family to New York.

After the firm broke up in 1907, Harmon knew what he wanted to do. "Some men keep a racing stable or a yacht," he said. "I have much more fun spending my money in helping people to help themselves."

Andrew Carnegie gave Lebanon $10,000 in 1906 toward the construction of a library. The following year, Harmon contributed $3,500 for the books and furnishings.

Then in 1911, Harmon purchased 88 acres in Lebanon to establish a playground. He had a concrete dam constructed over Turtle Creek to create a swimming hole and funded a baseball diamond, trap-shooting range, tennis courts, golf links, and a half-mile running track. It was the first of 119 Harmon Parks he would establish in 32 states across the nation.

In December 1912, construction began on Harmon Hall, an indoor

recreational facility. Located on Broadway next to the library, it now houses the Warren County Historical Society Museum. He also established the Harmon Civic Trust in 1915. This panel of Lebanon citizens, which still exists today, was organized to administer funds for "the improvement of the ... conditions of living in the town of Lebanon."

Harmon died on July 15, 1928, after suffering a mild heart attack in May. He had just dedicated the Mollie Harmon Home for Aged Gentlefolk on Mechanic Street, in honor of his mother. On a stone monument at Harmon Golf Club there is a plaque with a likeness of Harmon. On the bottom are his words: "Serving one's own people ... transcends duty ... and becomes a privilege."

25 Letters from the ghost of Jedediah Tingle

Jedediah Tingle, in 1797, was one of the earliest settlers to the Lebanon area. He died there in 1827. Nearly a century later, something very strange began to happen. People started to receive notes and gifts from a man who had been dead for years. They began to get letters from ... Jedediah Tingle.

Tingle was born in Delaware in 1767. When he was 30, he came to what is now Warren County. There he built a log cabin and planted the first apple orchard in this part of the country along what is now St. Rt. 123. Twenty years later Tingle built the brick house where he and his wife, Elizabeth, would raise their 15 children. His initials "J. T." and the year 1817 can be seen on the left hand side of the home today. Tingle died at age 61 and was buried in Lebanon's old Methodist Graveyard.

Nearly 100 years later, in 1921, the "Jedediah Tingle" letters began arriving. They were written on stationary that had a small sketch of a tombstone with the initials "J. T." on it. Jedediah's notes were usually complimentary, but could also be quite opinionated. He frequently gave gifts of money, books, and magazines subscriptions.

Jedediah gave funds and encouragement to a wide variety of organizations, including the American Committee for the Relief of German Children, the Jewish Relief, the Little Italy Neighborhood Home and the Exhibit of American Negro Art. Some of the more intriguing sounding groups to benefit were the Howard Mission and Home for Little Wanderers, the Working Girl's Vacation Society and the Association for Relief of Respectable, Aged, Indigent, Females.

Recipients of his letters and gifts were often ordinary citizens, like a heroic local policeman or a caring clergyman. Many, however, were famous and powerful people, such as the trailblazing female reporter Nellie Bly, movie star Charlie Chaplin, author Fannie Hurst, poet Edna St. Vincent Millay and General John J. Pershing. Presidents Wilson, Harding, and Coolidge all received letters as did then Secretary of Commerce Herbert Hoover. Vice President Charles G. Dawes received a pipe after winning the Nobel Peace Prize in 1925. Even Benito Mussolini received a book from Jedediah.

The famed deaf mute Helen Keller, after receiving a gift, wrote, "Dear Joy Bringer alias Jedediah Tingle, I am very grateful to you for your lovely gesture toward me, and for being interested in my endeavors. The way you say things is full of charm and reveals a lovely personality."

It wasn't until the death of a noted Lebanon native on July 15, 1928, that the author of the "Jedediah Tingle" letters was identified by *The New York Times*. "Jedediah Tingle, mysterious philanthropist, whose benefactions gladdened the hearts and lightened the cares of noted writers and obscure poets, unsung heroes and poor children for many years has been revealed as William Elmer Harmon."

Harmon was the Lebanon-born philanthropist who had given the village Harmon Hall, Harmon Park and the Harmon Civic Trust. He apparently also received great joy in helping others under the guise of his maternal great-grandfather, Jedediah Tingle. As "Jedediah," Harmon once wrote that he was carrying "on a mission to bring a smile and a tender thought in high and low places, to comfort and cheer those who do exceptional things or suffer."

26 Ashes to ashes: The Lebanon Opera House

It was called "the most disastrous fire in the history of Lebanon." On September 1, 1874, a blaze destroyed several buildings in the heart of the village, including the town hall and what was once the Ferguson House. Arising from these ashes, in 1878, was "the finest public building in Warren County" — the Lebanon Opera House. But no one knew that a similar fate awaited it.

The three-story Victorian Gothic structure, on the corner of Broadway and Main, housed the village council chamber and other government offices, including the jail. Its second floor featured a 1,200-seat auditorium, one of the "handsomest halls in the state." Speeches from Frederick Douglass, Elizabeth Cady Stanton, William McKinley and Warren G. Harding were delivered from the Opera House stage, as were a variety of theatrical performances.

It showed its first movie in 1918, and its last on Saturday, December 24, 1932. The final film was prophetically titled *Hot Saturday*. At 3:40 Christmas morning, Patrolman Grant Shaffer turned down the alley by the post office on Mulberry Street and saw smoke pouring from the Opera House.

Meanwhile, Congressman Charles Franklin West, of Granville, Ohio, was arriving in town to spend Christmas with relatives. He noticed an odd reflection in the Opera House windows and soon realized it was fire. Both men ran into the Canteen on Broadway simultaneously — Shaffer from the rear and West from the front. They told Clark South to notify the fire department.

Moments before, John Pluckett, at the village power plant, noticed the blaze and called it in. Officer Shaffer then rushed to the Opera House to "release a tramp who had sought refuge in the village lockup overnight."

Lebanon's fire department responded at once. Chief William Pflanzer quickly realized that saving the building was impossible. Keeping the fire from spreading was now the issue. The Mason and Franklin departments were called for assistance and arrived within one half hour. In the early minutes of the blaze, Mayor Ralph H. Carey and other officials repeatedly ran into the burning town hall to save village and township records.

A southerly wind carried burning embers toward surrounding buildings, setting ablaze the awning of Fred's Department Store on Mulberry Street. On the Masonic Temple roof, Marion Mulford used his coat sleeve to put out several small fires. Patrols watched for possible fires as far north as the French Creamery, one half mile away.

Flames engulfed the Opera House rapidly. At 4 a.m., the blackened, flame-

lit town clock struck the hour. By 4:08 it stood frozen. An hour later the clock tower tumbled into the blazing inferno. The fire was controlled by 5:30 a.m., but the Opera House was lost.

The source of the devastation was arson. Flammable movie film was used to start the fire backstage in the auditorium. Scorched film reels, ironically, were also found in the fire department, which was housed in the structure. The arsonist was never found.

Echoing the sentiment made over 50 years earlier after the previous town hall fire, *The Western Star* of December 29, 1932, declared it the "most destructive blaze in [the] history of Lebanon."

²⁷ Ronald Reagan's campaign for the 'heart of the Republican Party'

In its more than 200 years of existence, The Golden Lamb has seen more than its share of U.S. presidents. At the end of the 20th century, the portraits of 10 of the nation's chief executives graced the cover of its menu. They all visited the historic inn during its first 111 years. The eleventh presidential visitor, however, came more than 50 years later, and he would become one of the most beloved: Ronald Reagan.

The occasion for his visit was to aid the reelection campaign of freshman Congressman Donald E. "Buz" Lukens and the efforts of other Ohio Republican candidates.

Reagan was governor of California in 1968, and had been mentioned as a prospective presidential candidate by the Republican Party's conservative wing ever since his election two years earlier. Lukens had acted as his campaign manager at that summer's Republican National Convention in Miami Beach, Florida. The convention saw Reagan transform from California's "favorite son" into a full-fledged presidential candidate. He came in third for his party's nomination, behind Richard Nixon and Nelson Rockefeller.

Reagan arrived at about noon on September 19, 1968, at Middletown, Ohio's Hock Field, where he was greeted by 400 enthusiastic political supporters, movie fans and members of TAR, the Teenage Republicans. After a luncheon at the Manchester Inn, the governor and Lukens left for Lebanon. *The Western Star* reported that Lebanon Mayor Lou Romohr proclaimed it "Ronald Reagan Day" and that the "red carpet" was out for "the former actor and TV star."

At about 2 p.m., 100 "partisans" greeted the governor in The Golden Lamb's Black Horse Tavern, which in 1968 was located in the hotel's lower level. The microphone Reagan was supposed to use did not work. Seventeen-year-old bus boy Fred Compton quickly got the governor a Windsor chair upon which to stand.

From this high perch, Reagan called Lukens "the best legislator I have ever seen and the most deserving of your support." He admitted he was in Ohio to repay Lukens for his hard work at the Republican convention.

"We've known each other a long time," he recalled. "In fact, we've known each other since we were both Democrats — before the party leadership left us."

"I wonder what the 10 Commandments would have been like if Moses had to run them through a Democratic legislature," Reagan said with a smile.

Before leaving, he made it a point to shake the hand of everyone in the room. Reagan then made brief stops in Hamilton and Fairfield. That night he spoke at a $1,000-a-plate fund-raising dinner in Cincinnati.

Compton remembers Reagan calling Lukens "the heart of the Republican Party and the hope of the future."

Lukens did not live up to that high praise. In the 1980s and '90s he was involved in numerous scandals, indicted and eventually imprisoned. For many Americans, however, Reagan's words would more aptly apply to another. To them "the heart of the Republican Party and the hope of the future" was none other than Ronald Reagan.

28 Lebanon's portrayal of 'the All-American town'

Throughout its history Lebanon has been a pioneer village, a college town and a county seat. In the fall of 1977 it played one of its more interesting "roles." For two weeks that October, Lebanon "went Hollywood" and pretended it was Harper Valley, Ohio.

The occasion was the filming of *Harper Valley PTA*, a motion picture based on the 1968 country hit. It told the story of Stella Johnson, a "Harper Valley widowed wife." The PTA felt Stella's dresses were "way too high" and her "runnin' round" inappropriate and took it out on her daughter. Stella then took revenge on these "Harper Valley hypocrites."

Some Lebanon citizens were concerned that the town was chosen because it "depicted the double standards found in many of the country's smaller communities." Executive producer Phil Borak — who was no stranger to Lebanon, having once owned the Old Fort Drive-in Theater on Columbus Avenue — said, "No. Lebanon was selected because it's so picturesque. It fit my image of what a pretty small town in America should look like."

The movie starred Barbara Eden of television's *I Dream of Jeannie* fame and featured such well-known comedic actors as Nanette Fabray, Louis Nye and Pat Paulsen.

The comedy used several Lebanon locations. Berry Middle School doubled as Harper Valley High. Several scenes were filmed there, including one showing students being dismissed. About 200 high schoolers "acted" all afternoon as Berry's students sat in their classrooms behind drawn shades. Interior and exterior scenes were filmed at The Village Ice Cream Parlor as well as "The Pillars" mansion on Cincinnati Avenue. A two-story house on Deerfield Road portrayed the Johnson home. Set director Tom Rusmussen spent more than an hour placing what he jokingly called "artistic (toilet) paper" on the house and its trees for one scene.

Of all the local performers, 19-year-old Brian Cook had the biggest part, playing the boyfriend of Stella's daughter.

On May 24, 1978, at the Lebanon premiere of the film at the Colony Square Cinema, the biggest cheer was for another local "actor." Herschel Kendrick played a farmer hauling hay on Markey Road. The uproar occurred when the movie's heavies plowed into his load of hay while chasing Eden and Fabray.

The opening and closing credits were the film's most beautiful segments.

They showed scenic helicopter shots of Lebanon and the surrounding country.

The acting bug struck Lebanon again in 1993 with the filming of *Milk Money*. Like *Harper Valley PTA*, it was filmed in October, had scenes in The Village Ice Cream Parlor and told the story of a blonde of questionable reputation. This time she was played by Melanie Griffith. Lebanon had to stretch its acting skills for this role. It now portrayed Middleton, Pennsylvania, and had to pretend cold October nights were actually balmy summer evenings.

"I pictured in my mind a small, Midwestern, Norman Rockwellish town," said screenwriter John Mattson. "Lebanon is that town. Just look around, the shops, restaurants — it's all here. This is the All-American town."

29 The first 'sitting' president to stand before The Golden Lamb

As managing partner of The Golden Lamb, Paul Resetar felt something special was needed to mark the hotel's 200th anniversary in 2003. So he wrote to President George W. Bush on May 18, 2002, and invited him to join the ranks of the 11 other chief executives who had visited Ohio's oldest inn.

After several contacts, the White House finally said "yes" in early April 2004. The president would come as part of his "Yes, America Can" re-election campaign tour of Ohio.

On the morning of May 4, 2004, a four-block area of downtown was sealed off in preparation for Bush's arrival at 2:30 p.m.

At 11:30 a.m., the first of the partisan crowd began to pass through metal detectors on the north side of the city building. 2,500 tickets were printed for the event, but more than 4,500 were requested. During the three-hour wait, the Lebanon High School Band and other local talents performed. Former Cincinnati Bengal Anthony Munoz acted as master of ceremonies, and Rep. Rob Portman (R-Cincinnati) and Mayor Amy Brewer gave brief speeches.

Burly secret service agents, dressed in black fatigues and carrying high-powered binoculars and weapons, stood on the hotel's roof.

At 2:37 p.m. a 14-vehicle caravan approached from W. Main Street. A lone red, white and blue bus turned left onto Broadway, stopping in front of the hotel. A few minutes later, Bush emerged and walked toward the platform in front of the hotel.

Portman exclaimed, "There has never been . . . a more important visitor to Lebanon, Ohio and The Golden Lamb."

As the congressman spoke, Bush, jacketless and wearing a cowboy belt with his dress shirt and tie, waved to the crowd.

In his opening remarks, Bush said, "I am proud to be the first sitting president to have visited here – actually I'm a standing president today." He called Portman a "fine congressman," adding, "I didn't know he was an innkeeper," referring to Portman's family owning The Golden Lamb building. Bush thanked Brewer for "her service" after jokingly advising her to "fill the potholes, mayor." It was a line he used at several campaign stops.

Speaking for almost 30 minutes, he ended by praising Linda Rabolt's work with the homeless in Lebanon's Interfaith Hospitality Network stating, "That's the spirit of this country."

For the next 15 minutes the president shook hands and signed autographs.

When Bush walked into The Golden Lamb, Resetar was thrilled. He was struck by how "comfortable" the president seemed.

Resetar showed him the second-floor guest room that would be renamed the "George W. Bush Room." It is the room in which the president's mother, Barbara Bush, stayed on April 12, 1988.

Bush soon returned to his bus and the caravan drove on to Cincinnati.

Today, over the fireplace in the hotel lobby, there is a 3-by-4-foot shadow-box frame of mementos from the president's visit. Amid the buttons, flags and photos is a letter from Bush dated May 11, 2004.

He writes, "It is an honor to be the first sitting President to visit the Golden Lamb Inn and I am proud to have a room named after me in such a legendary and treasured landmark."

Selected bibliography

The records and resources of the Warren County Historical Society Museum library in Lebanon were used extensively, including various microfilmed editions of *The Western Star* newspaper from 1807 through 2004. Other sources include:

Andrews, Edward Deming. *The People Called Shaker*. New York: Dover, 1963.

Bochin, Hal W. "Tom Corwin's Speech against the Mexican War: Courageous But Misunderstood." *Ohio History* 90 (Autumn 1981): 33–53.

Boller, Paul F. Jr. *Congressional Anecdotes*. New York: Oxford University Press, 1991.

Brooks, Tim, and Earle Marsh. *The Complete Directory to Prime Time Network TV Shows: 1946–Present*. 5th ed. New York: Ballantine Books, 1992.

Centennial Atlas of Warren County, Ohio, The. Lebanon, Ohio: The Centennial Atlas Association, 1903.

Dickens, Charles. *American Notes*. New York: The Modern Library, 1996.

_____. *A Christmas Carol: A Ghost Story of Christmas*. Ed. Michael Slater. Boston: Otter Books, 1991.

Havighurst, Walter. *The Miami Years*. New York: G.P. Putnam's Sons, 1958.

History of Warren County, Ohio, The. Chicago: W.H. Beers & Co., 1882.

Hopkins, James F. et al. eds. *The Papers of Henry Clay: Vol. 4, Secretary of State, 1825.*, Lexington, Kentucky: The University Press of Kentucky, 1973.

Howe, Henry. *Historical Collections of Ohio*. Cincinnati, Ohio: C.J. Krehbiel & Co., 1902.

Kay, Karl J. *History of the National Normal University of Lebanon, Ohio*. Wilmington, Ohio: Wilmington College, 1929.

Phillips, Hazel Spencer. *Banking in Warren County, Ohio*. Oxford, Ohio: The Oxford Press, 1960.

_____. *The Golden Lamb*. Oxford, Ohio: The Oxford Press, 1958.

_____. *Richard the Shaker*. Oxford, Ohio: Typoprint, 1972.

_____. *To Serve a People Is a Divine Privilege: William Elmer Harmon*. Lebanon, Ohio: The Harmon Civic Trust, n.d.

Purvis, Dennis, and Matt Cole. "Milk Money: Hollywood Comes to Lebanon." *Lebanon Light*. 5 November 1993, 8.

Riley, Jeannie C. "Harper Valley P.T.A." *Harper Valley P.T.A.* Plantation, PLP 1,1968.

Shriver, Phillip R. *Miami University: A Personal History*. Ed. William Pratt. Oxford, Ohio: Miami University Press, 1998.

Siebert, Wilbur H. *The Mysteries of Ohio's Underground Railroads*. Columbus, Ohio: Long's College Book Company, 1951.

_____ . *The Underground Railroad: From Slavery to Freedom*. New York: The MacMillan Company, 1898.

Venable, William H., "The Lebanon Centennial," *Ohio Archaeological and Historical Quarterly* 11 (October 1902): 198–214.